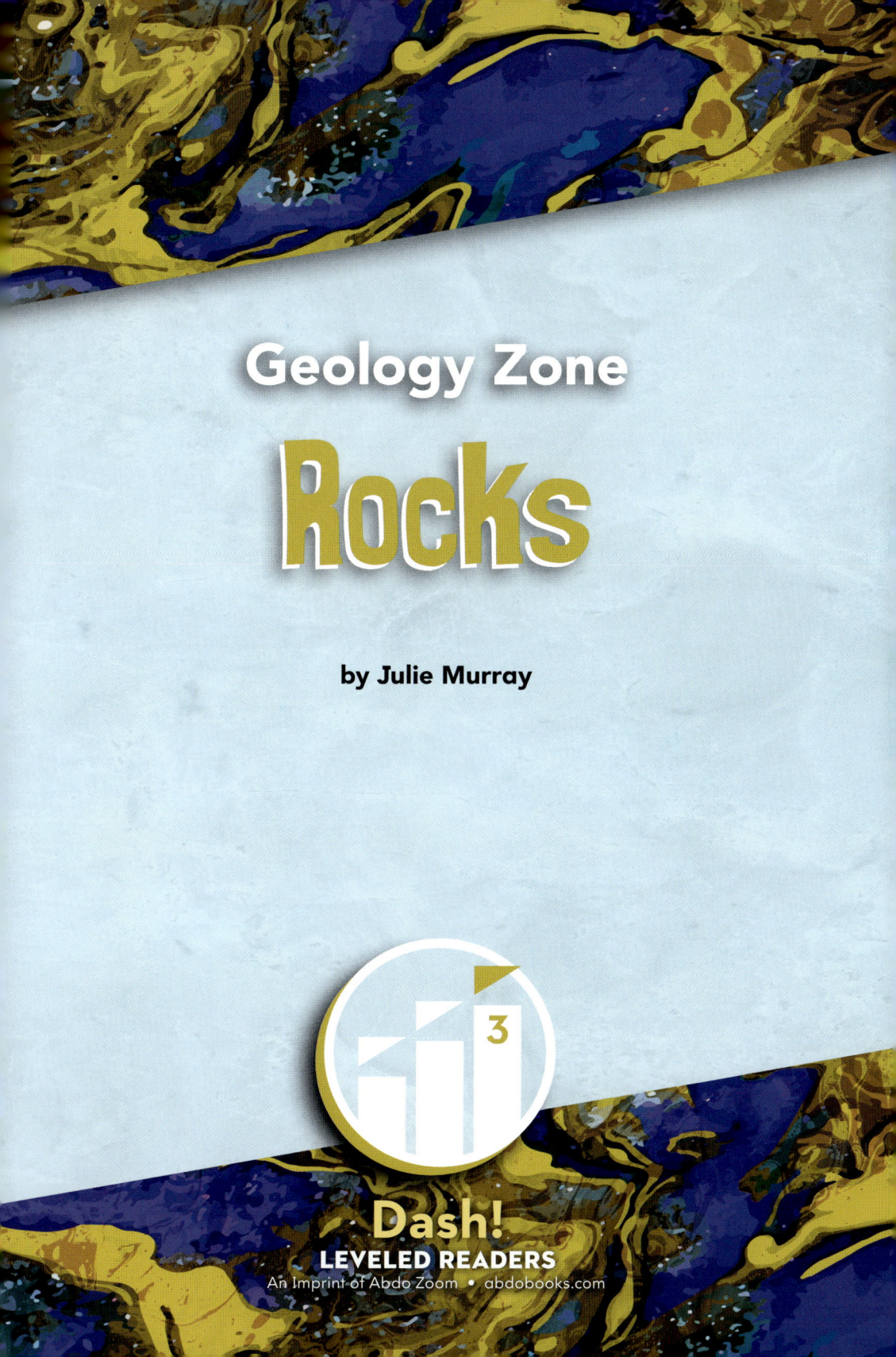

Level 1 – Beginning
Short and simple sentences with familiar words or patterns for children who are beginning to understand how letters and sounds go together.

Level 2 – Emerging
Longer words and sentences with more complex language patterns for readers who are practicing common words and letter sounds.

Level 3 – Transitional
More developed language and vocabulary for readers who are becoming more independent.

THIS BOOK CONTAINS RECYCLED MATERIALS

abdobooks.com

Published by Abdo Zoom, a division of ABDO, PO Box 398166, Minneapolis, Minnesota 55439. Copyright © 2025 by Abdo Consulting Group, Inc. International copyrights reserved in all countries. No part of this book may be reproduced in any form without written permission from the publisher. Dash!™ is a trademark and logo of Abdo Zoom.

Printed in the United States of America, North Mankato, Minnesota.
102024
012025

Photo Credits: Getty Images, Shutterstock
Production Contributors: Kenny Abdo, Jennie Forsberg, Grace Hansen, John Hansen
Design Contributors: Candice Keimig, Neil Klinepier

Library of Congress Control Number: 2024936542

Publisher's Cataloging in Publication Data
Names: Murray, Julie, author.
Title: Rocks / by Julie Murray
Description: Minneapolis, Minnesota : Abdo Zoom, 2025 | Series: Geology zone | Includes online resources and index.
Identifiers: ISBN 9781098287191 (lib. bdg.) | ISBN 9781098287894 (ebook) | ISBN 9781098288242 (Read-to-me ebook)
Subjects: LCSH: Rocks--Juvenile literature. | Geology--Juvenile literature. | Rocks--Identification--Juvenile literature. | Earth sciences--Juvenile literature.
Classification: DDC 552--dc23

Table of Contents

Rocks 4

Kinds of Rocks 6

Uses of Rocks 16

More Facts 22

Glossary 23

Index 24

Online Resources 24

Rocks

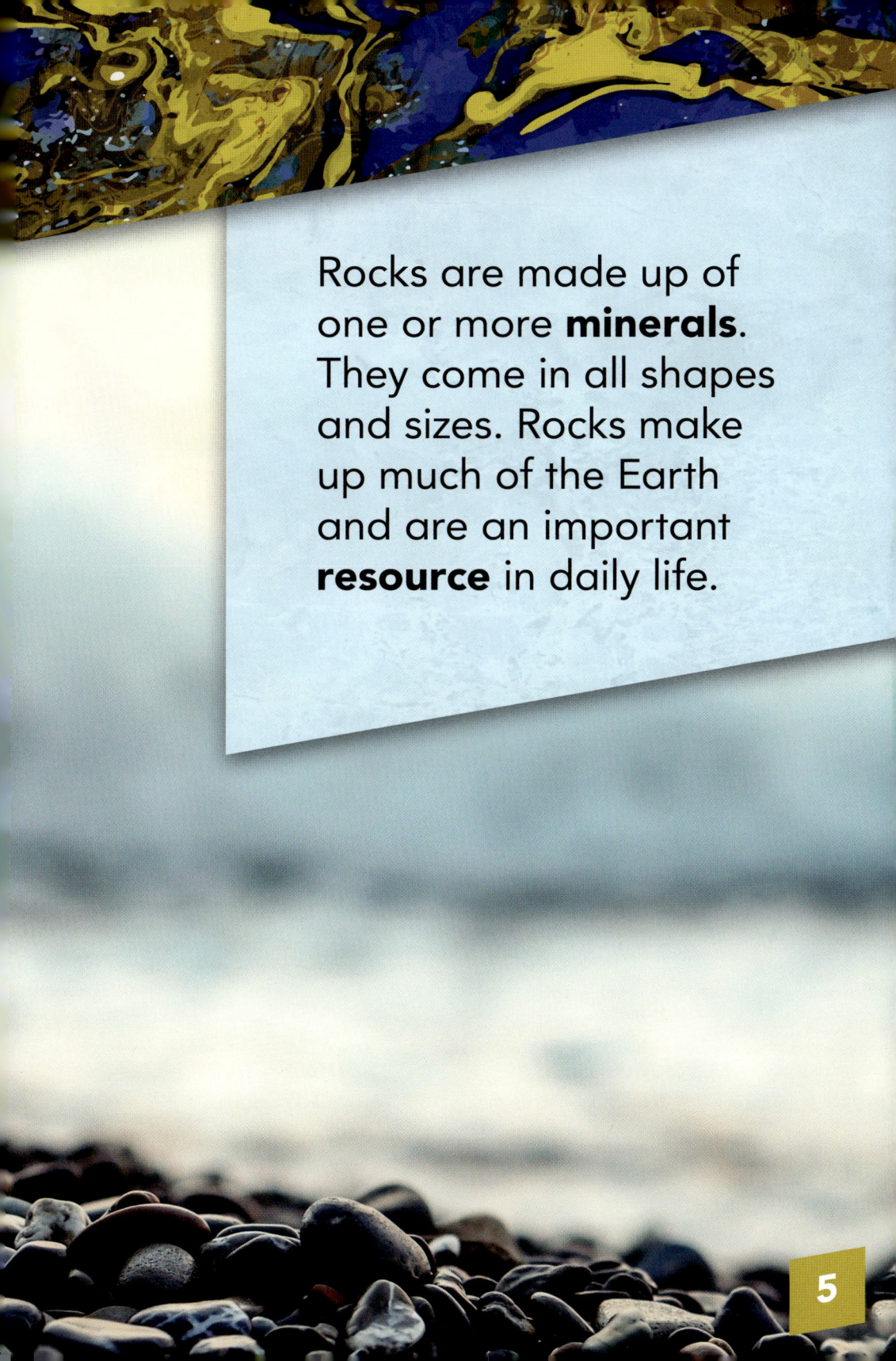

Rocks are made up of one or more **minerals**. They come in all shapes and sizes. Rocks make up much of the Earth and are an important **resource** in daily life.

Kinds of Rocks

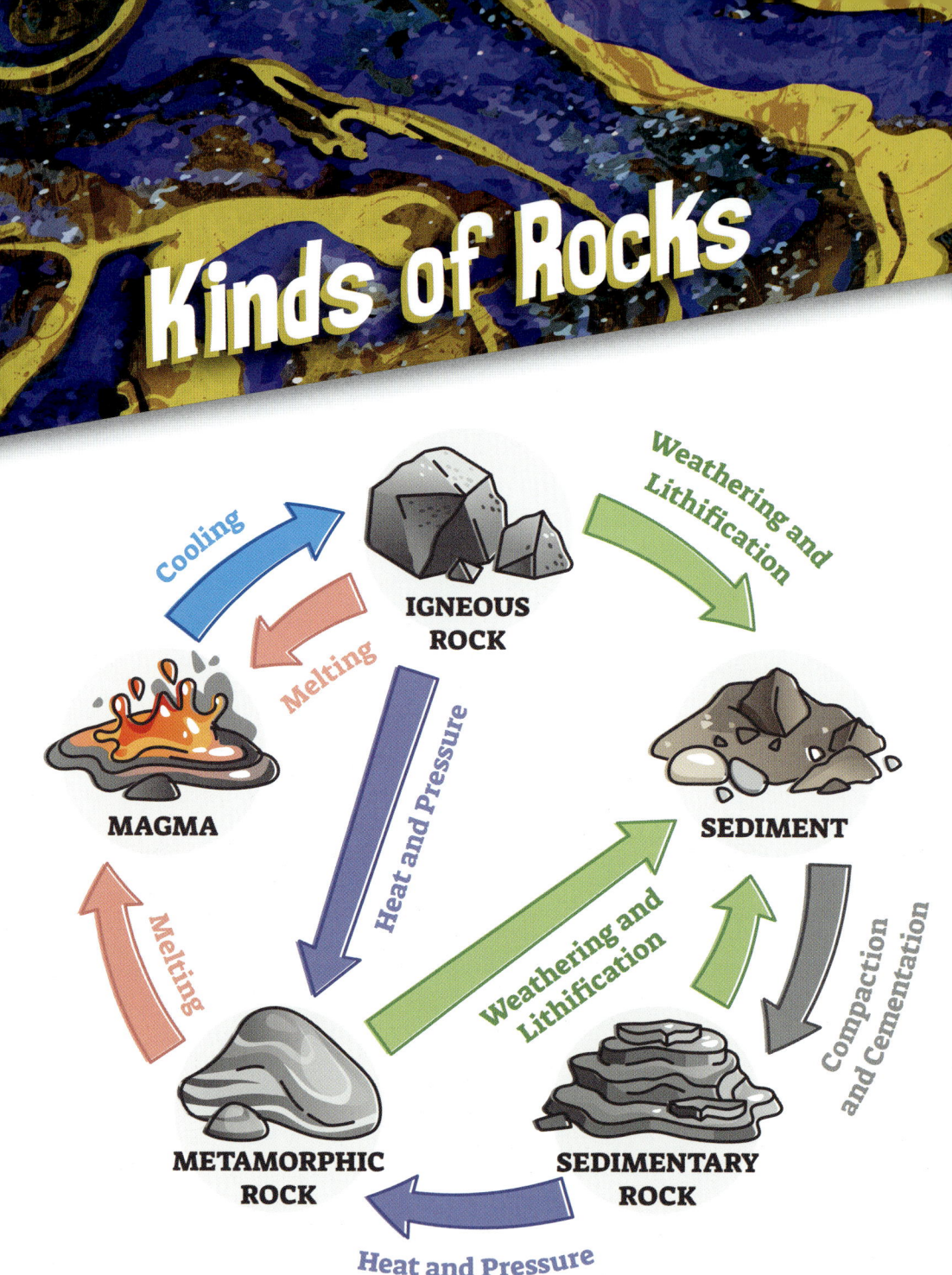

ROCK CYCLE

There are three kinds of rock: sedimentary, metamorphic, and igneous. They form in different ways.

Sedimentary

Metamorphic

Igneous

Igneous rock forms when magma cools above or below Earth's **crust**. The magma rises and hardens into rock. Granite is formed this way.

Sedimentary rock forms from tiny rocks that pile together to make layers. The weight creates **pressure** and forms one large rock. Limestone is made this way.

The Grand Canyon is made up of many rock layers. Each layer was formed at a different time. The deepest layers were formed 1.8 billion years ago!

Metamorphic rock forms from igneous or sedimentary rock that changed under high heat and high **pressure**. Marble forms when limestone rock is heated to very high temperatures.

Uses of Rocks

Humans have used rocks for millions of years. Rocks were once used to make weapons. They were also used to make tools for chopping, digging, and cutting.

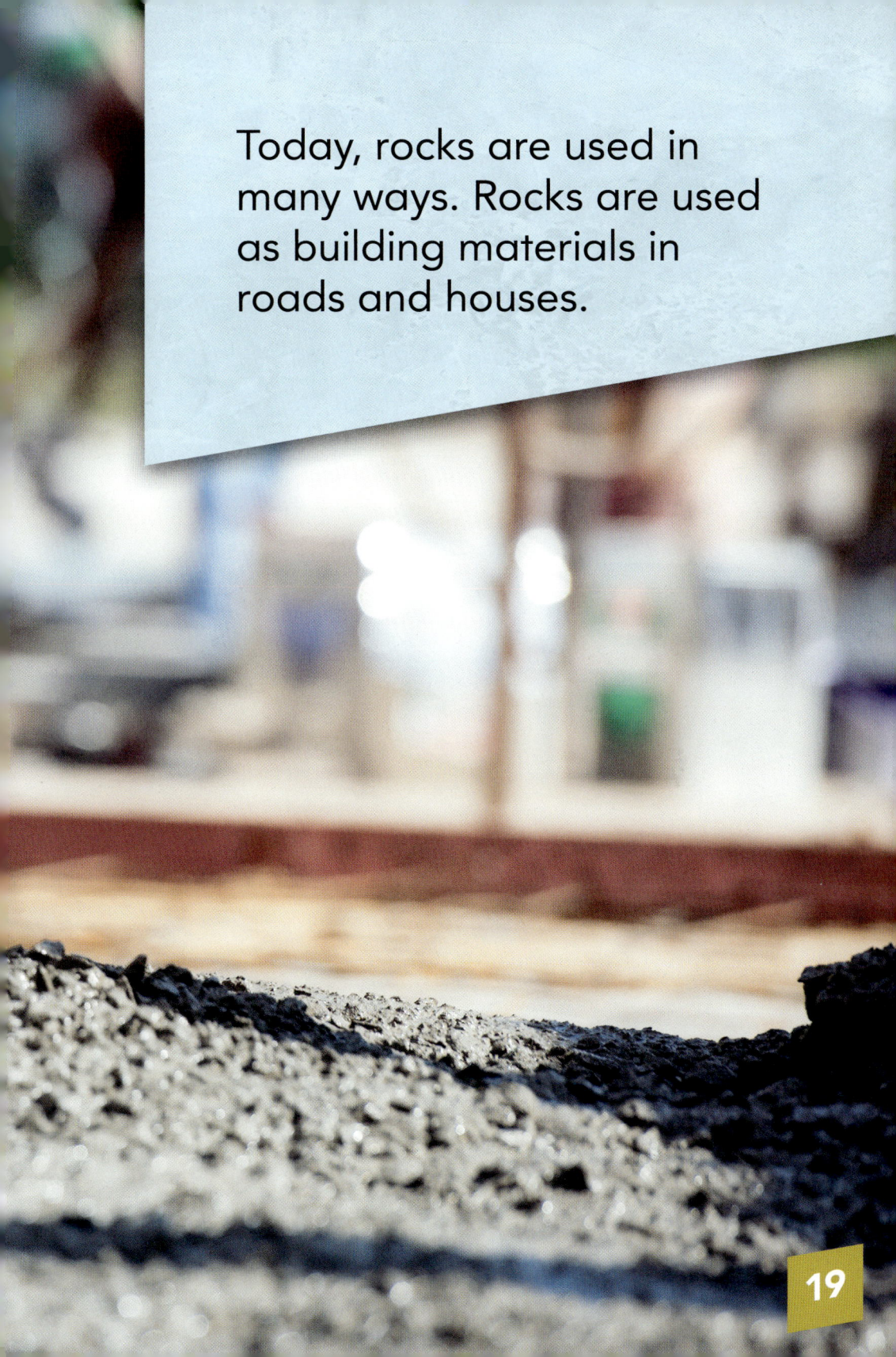

Today, rocks are used in many ways. Rocks are used as building materials in roads and houses.

Minerals that are found in rocks are also used. Aluminum is used to make soda cans. Copper is used to make electrical wires.

More Facts

- Geology is the study of rocks. Scientists who study rocks are called geologists.

- Rocks from space can land on Earth. These rocks are called meteorites.

- Glass, pennies, and salt are all products made from rocks.

Glossary

crust – the outer layer of Earth.

mineral – a substance formed in the earth that is not of an animal or a plant.

pressure – a steady force upon a surface.

resource – a natural feature that enhances the quality of human life.

Index

cans 21
construction 19
electrical wires 20
formation 7, 9, 11, 12, 15
Grand Canyon 12
igneous 7, 9

metamorphic 7, 15
minerals 5, 20
roads 19
sedimentary 7, 11, 12
tools 16
weapons 16

Online Resources

To learn more about rocks, please visit **abdobooklinks.com** or scan this QR code. These links are routinely monitored and updated to provide the most current information available.